Let's Take a Trip
A River Adventure

by Patricia Griffith Morgan
photography by Michael Plunkett

Troll Associates

Library of Congress Cataloging in Publication Data

Morgan, Patricia Griffith.
  A river adventure.

  (Let's take a trip)
  Summary: Follows a group of canoeists as they
explore and enjoy ninety-two miles of waterway along
the Allagash River in northern Maine.
    1. Canoes and canoeing—Maine—Allagash River—
Juvenile literature. 2. Allagash River (Me.)—
Description and travel—Juvenile literature.
[1. Canoes and canoeing—Maine—Allagash River.
2. Allagash River (Me.)—Description and travel]
I. Plunkett, Michael, ill. II. Title.
GV776.M22A445   1988   917.41   87-3485
ISBN 0-8167-1171-2 (lib. bdg.)
ISBN 0-8167-1172-0 (pbk.)

The author and publisher wish to thank Warren Cochrane, Chip Cochrane and Linda Koski of the Allagash Canoe
Trips for their generous assistance and cooperation; and to acknowledge Fred L. Knapp for the inset photographs on
pages 24 and 25.

Thousands of people visit northern Maine with one special challenge in mind. They come to hike, canoe, and camp out along the Allagash Wilderness Waterway. It takes a week to travel the ninety-two miles of the waterway. Let's join one group of canoeists for a trip down the Allagash River!

First, the group must register with the Maine State Park Rangers. It's important for the rangers to know how many people are in each park or wilderness area. They also need a list of names in case they must locate someone. Chip Cochrane, the leader of the group, signs them in at the ranger station.

Everyone helps get the canoes into the water. Each person is given a paddle that is right for his or her own height. Then the gear is loaded into the canoes. Each canoe must be equipped with a life jacket for each passenger. Chip and his assistant, Cindy, lift a wooden box, or *wannigan,* into a canoe. The wannigan is used to store food.

Before they head down Indian Stream, Chip demonstrates basic paddling strokes. The group will build up their paddling time, a little bit each day, until they are comfortable with the feel of the canoe and paddling through the water.

And they're off! The Allagash River is a body of water that connects many lakes, ponds, and streams. Together they form the Allagash Wilderness Waterway, a part of the Great North Woods. The waterway and the land on each side of it are protected by the Wilderness Act. Logging and other industry are forbidden in this part of the woods.

But years ago, whole areas of the forest were cut down by timber companies. Steam engines carried logs down the railway from Eagle Lake to another lake. From there, the logs were floated downstream to mills to be made into paper. The canoeists come ashore on Eagle Lake to explore a rusty old engine. They know that, today, logs are transported on the backs of flatbed trucks.

Another favorite spot on Eagle Lake is a rest stop known as Farm Island. Here some members of the group relax. Others swim and explore. Still others enjoy jumping from high cliffs into the cool blue lake. This is lots of fun, especially after paddling for awhile on a hot summer day.

And there's more excitement in store for the group as they paddle around the bend. Although you aren't likely to see an animal out in the hot midday sun, the lucky canoeists have discovered a moose who's discovered a way to cool off!

Many wild animals can be seen along the Allagash, including the white-tailed deer. The canoeists spot a deer browsing along the shoreline—probably searching for food.

And, speaking of food, it's just about time to set up camp and have dinner. The campers pitch their tents carefully—so they won't collapse during the night! A *ground cloth* is placed at the base of each tent to keep out the dampness and rain. Then, one, two, three ... up goes the tent!

Soon it is time for dinner. Chip puts a pan of cake batter into a *reflector oven*. He places it in front of the campfire, where the other food is cooking. The metal oven reflects the heat, and the heat from the fire bakes the cake. When dinner is ready, two campers decide to dine in a shady spot!

The next morning they arrive at Churchill
Dam, which was once used for logs cut during
the winter. The dam held back the water and
the logs until the river ice thawed in the
spring. Then the gates of the dam were opened
up, and the rushing water carried the logs
downstream to the paper mills.

At Churchill Dam the adventurers have to carry their canoes across a narrow strip of land. Then they can put back in the river below the dam to go on to the next lake. This is called *portage,* and it often occurs around dams and waterfalls. On the lake a brisk wind is blowing. One canoeist turns a ground cloth into a sail and takes a brief rest from paddling.

At Chase Rapids, the Allagash River runs very swiftly. Canoeists must be especially careful of the rocks half-hidden by the water. The smallest paddler stands, so he can see the rocks and pick a path between them. Cindy keeps an eye on her charge to be sure he can keep his balance!

After the excitement of the rapids, Chip leads
the group through the quiet backwater. He
guides his canoe through the shallow water
with a long setting pole. This is called *poling*.
It is one of the few times that standing in a canoe
is allowed!

Although bushes and trees and all forms of plant life were once destroyed when lumber was harvested, the Wilderness Act has preserved forests along the waterway, so plant life now abounds there. Bright red *bunchberries* poke out of green leaves, and the forests are filled with *ferns*.

There are many kinds of wild mushrooms along the Allagash, too. Some are good to eat, but others are poisonous—so it's best not to eat wild mushrooms! One type of mushroom is called *Indian pipe*. Can you see how it got its name?

At Ledges Campground, everyone sets up camp for another night. Tents are pitched, clothes are hung to dry, and fresh drinking water is drawn from the river. There's even time for a quick shampoo before the sun goes down. Water is warmed in a plastic pouch by the sun for an outdoor *sun shower.*

Chip chops kindling with an ax. Then he shows campers how to use the saw. When he's sure they can handle it safely, he lets them take over. Soon he has enough wood to fill the fireplace at the campsite. He lights the fire and gets dinner started.

This small grove of spruce trees at Ledges Campground is probably very old. Somehow it escaped the lumberman's ax during the old logging days! Today it is protected by the Wilderness Act, so it cannot be cut down. The campers enjoy this beautiful sight as they take a late afternoon walk.

Umsaskis Lake is the next link in the chain of the waterway. It is almost dreamlike as the paddlers glide through the early morning mist. They are reflected in the still water as if it were a mirror. Sunlight peeks through the trees. It's the start of another beautiful day as the paddlers head toward Long Lake.

An osprey swoops down to catch a fish it has
spotted in the water. It plunges into the water
and grabs the fish in its claws. The osprey,
also known as the *fish hawk,* has a wingspan of
as much as six feet. As soon as it captures its
prey in its claws, it rises back into the air.

As the paddlers glide around Long Lake, they spot a pair of *loons*. These diving water birds look somewhat like ducks. They mainly live on fish. Loons are a symbol for many people of the unspoiled wilderness. Their musical cry is often heard echoing across the lakes.

Long Lake Dam was an old logging dam where a rock wall and wooden gates once formed a *sluice*. The dam held back water, except through its narrow opening, or *sluiceway*. As the dammed-up water rushed through the sluiceway, it carried logs swiftly downstream.

The river still runs very fast here, and rocks are hidden underwater. The canoeists have to be careful, since a rock can easily put a hole in their canoe. Chip gets into the water to guide the canoe safely through.

The week of learning, exploring, and playing is nearly at an end. But these bold adventurers take time out to swim near the Allagash Falls. Chip leads the way as each one dives into the rugged water.

Final portage around the falls brings them closer to the end of their journey. Now it's just a short paddle to the little town where this wilderness adventure will end. Perhaps they'll return to the Allagash River for another adventure next year.

Though you're far from TV, you won't miss it at all! There are so many fun things to do—

like fishing in the lake, diving off the rocks, fooling around in the water, sun-bathing in a canoe, or relaxing in a hammock.

And, best of all, you can *share* the fun of a trip
down the river with friends.